You are Valued
   You are Worthy
      You are Loved

Poppins

Do you ever feel invisible... not seen or heard.

When you open up to say something....

Somebody talks over you like you are
not even there.

So you quietly sit back and listen
to all the endless chatter.

Then somebody whispers to you...
your voice really matters.

Do you look into a mirror and see
endless flaws.

The reflection looking back at you
judges you so harshly.

**Negative words you believe
about yourself take over your mind**

Then somebody whispers to you...
I love you just the way that you are.

Some days you feel you are on top of
the world. You move freely through
every obstacle.

There isn't anything that can get in your way.
Today you chose to be happy.

Good vibes seem to vanish quickly,
you get trapped into negative energy.

When one bad day turns into another,
you doubt you will feel happy again.

Then from out of the shadows a voice whispers to you... Turn your worries and hurt over to me.

Don't give up, whatever you do.

You must decide it's up to you to have a better attitude.

Life is beautifully messy at times.
Something to always be thankful for.

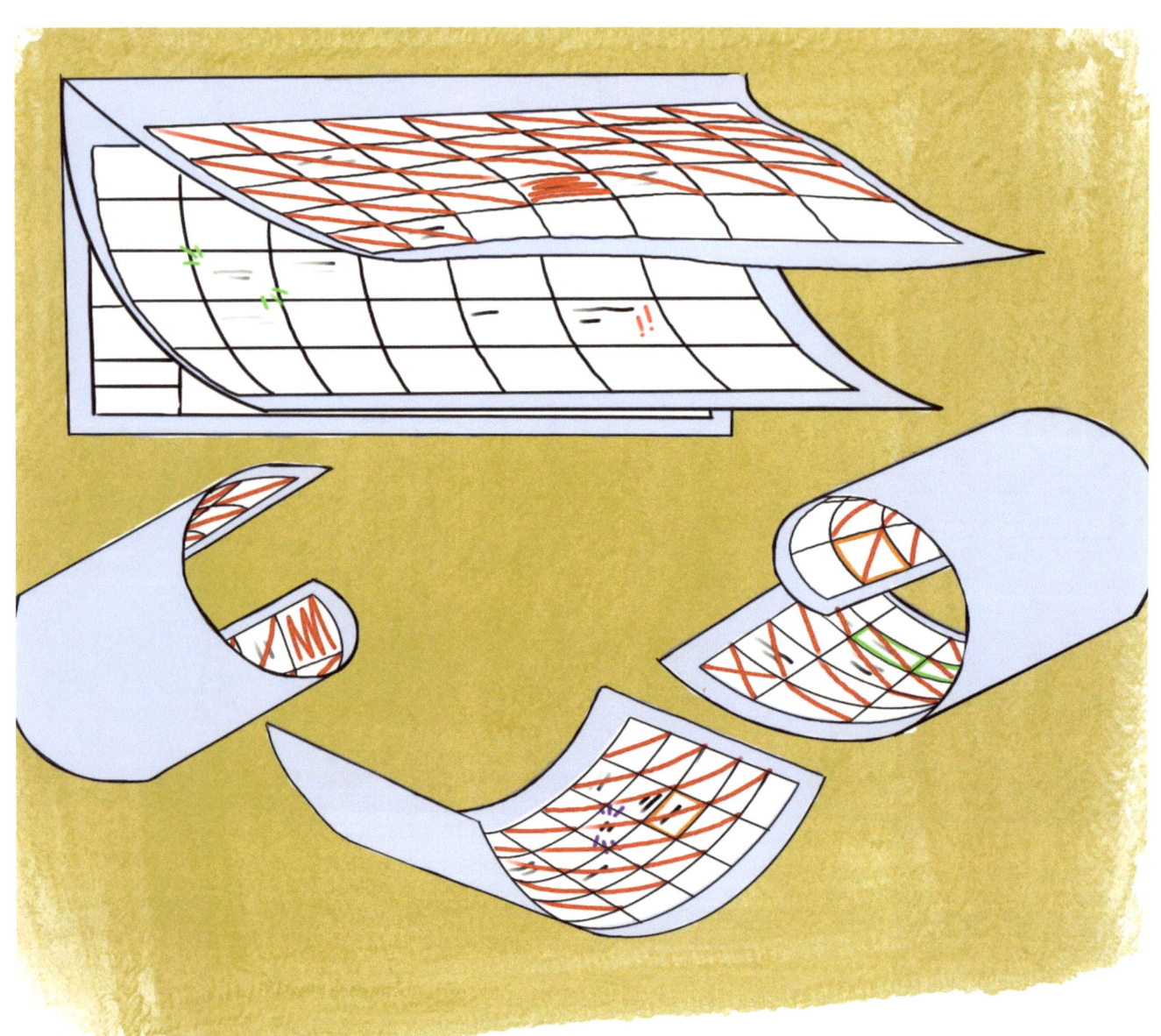

Days will go by whether you are happy
or sad. Not everyday will be fantastic.

Perfection in life posted on social media can make us doubt our own self worth.

So we try to create a flawless picture.
Then no one can see the real emotions
hidden within us

We are all struggling to be our true selves.

Then somebody whispers to you...
Stop trying to be somebody else.

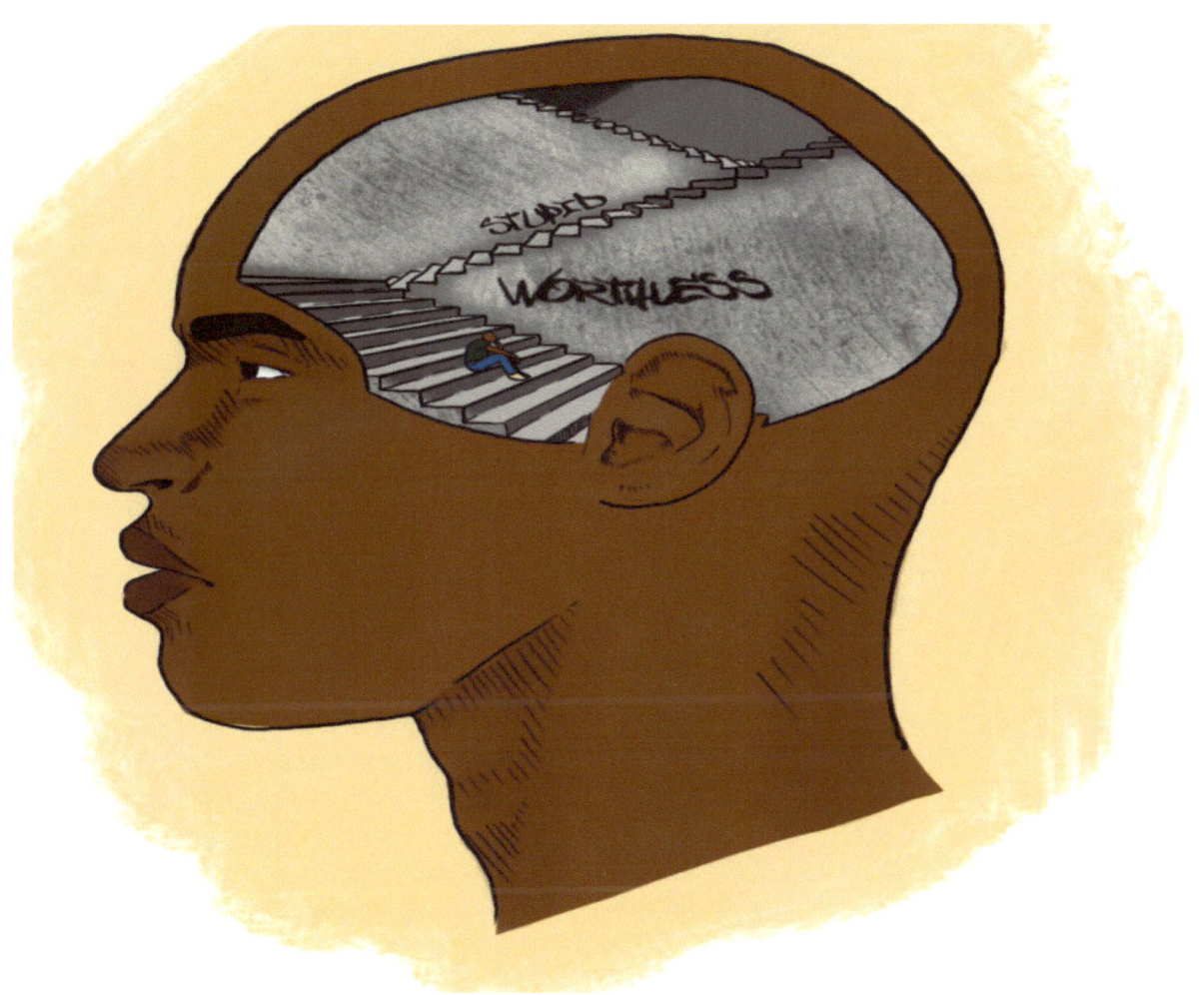

Negative messages get stuck in your head. You will never be good enough or quite measure up.

Hopeless and broken seem to define
how you feel.

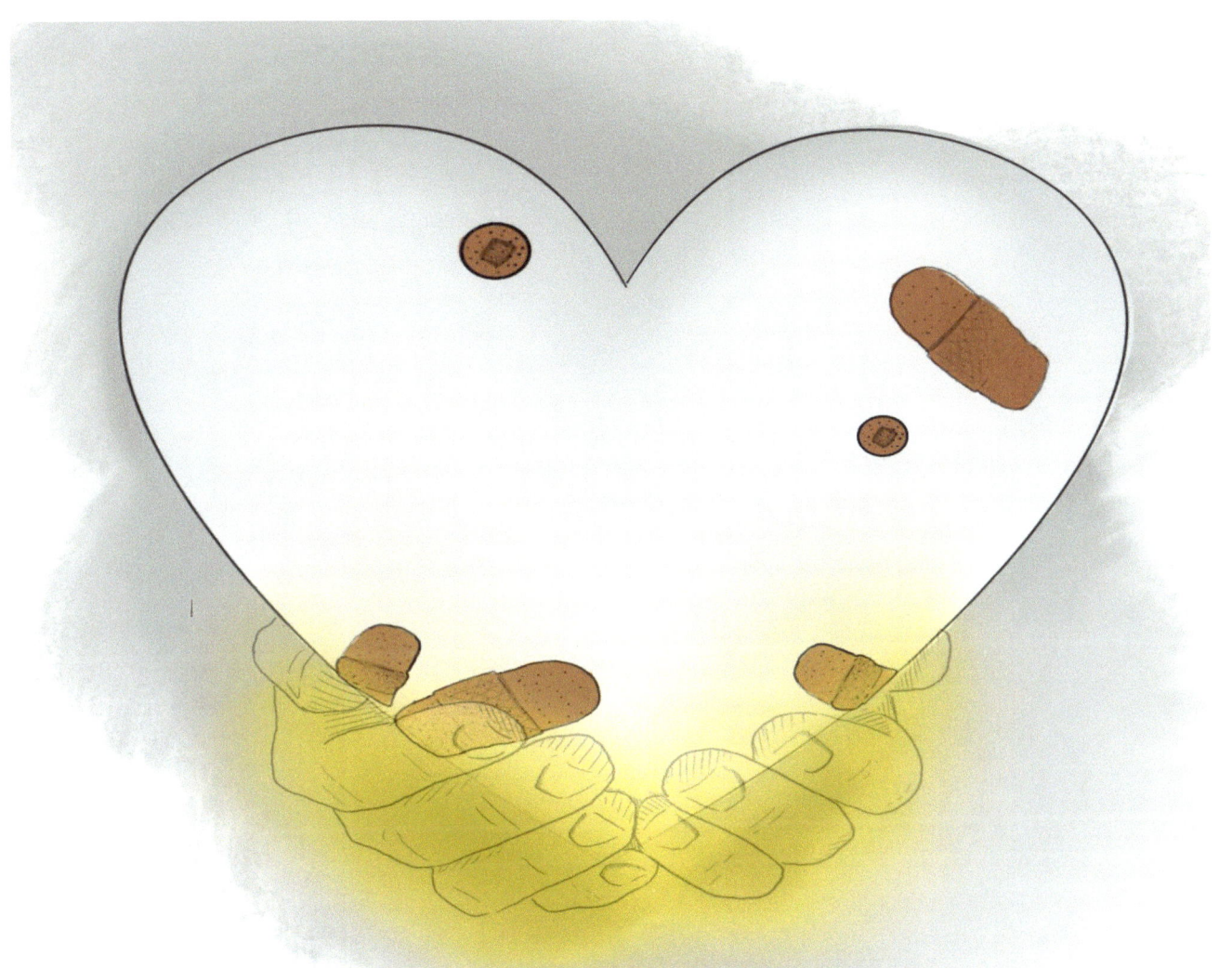

When a voice from the darkness whispers to you... You are more than enough just the way that you are.

Listen, you can hear

God's whisper

In the Breeze

Have Faith that life will get better. Have Hope for a better tomorrow. Carry Love in your heart for yourself. So you can show love and compassion for somebody else.

Y.O.U. Y.O.U

YOU

ONLY

UNDERESTIMATE

YOUR

OWN

UNIQUENESS